NATIONAL GEOGRAPHIC

Desert Rain

Pat Malone

This is a dry lake bed in a desert.
It hardly ever rains here.

2

But when it does rain, this dry lake bed
fills with water.
After a week of rain, the dry lake bed
becomes a lake.

Wildflowers spring up around the lake.
Their seeds have been in the ground,
waiting for rain.

4

Rivers run into the lake.
Fish swim into the lake from the rivers.

Pelicans come to the lake,
happy to find fish to eat.

More birds arrive.
All the birds have come to lay their eggs.

Desert shrubs burst into flower.

Spiders spin their webs everywhere.
They want to catch as many insects as they can.

9

After a few weeks, the pelicans take their babies down to the shore.
Soon the baby pelicans will learn to fly.

Then the water in the lake slowly starts to dry up.
Without water, the fish die.
The birds fly away in search of other food.

Then, one day, the lake is gone.

12

Without water, the flowers start to die.
But first they drop their seeds
for when the next rain comes.

13

When the rain comes,
this lake will fill up with water again.

Then the fish and the birds will return,
and this dry lake bed will be full of life once more.

Glossary

desert	a large area of dry land
lake	a large area of water surrounded by land
lake bed	the bottom of a lake
seed	the part of a plant that can grow into a new plant
shrub	a woody plant that is smaller than a tree
wildflowers	flowers that grow wild in a place